belvedere

GALLERY
GUIDE

ENGLISH

BELVEDERE
Baroque Palace and Art Collection

Salomon Kleiner, Prospect of Prince Eugene's gardens, neighbouring gardens of the St. Francis de Sales Monastery and Prince Schwarzenberg, etching, 1731

The Belvedere is an extensive Baroque palace complex comprising the Upper Belvedere, Lower Belvedere, Orangerie and Grand Stables buildings which are couched in magnificent Baroque gardens. The estate extends over gently sloping grounds and is adorned with cascades of staircase fountains, Baroque sculptures and splendid wrought iron gates. Since 1903, the palace estate has housed one of Austria's largest art museums. The collection focuses on works from Austria extending from the Middle Ages to contemporary pieces. The Belvedere is renowned as guardian of the world's largest collection of paintings by Gustav Klimt; it also houses one of the largest collections of Egon Schiele and Oskar Kokoschka paintings.

The Baroque estate of the Belvedere was originally conceived as a summer residence. At the time it was built, it was part of a general building boom in Vienna, the Imperial Emperor's residence, which was to bestow upon the city some of its most beautiful buildings. This prosperous era was made possible by the successful conclusion of the wars against the Ottoman Empire. After their unsuccessful siege of Vienna for several months in 1683, the Turks were pushed further and further eastwards before being ultimately crushed at the battle of Zenta in 1697. The commander of this important victory was Prince Eugene of Savoy, who commissioned the building of the Belvedere palaces.

Prince Eugene (Eugène François) was born in Paris in 1663 as the youngest of five sons. His father, Eugène-Maurice, Prince of Savoy-Carignan and Count of Soissons, hailed from a lateral branch of the reigning dukes of Savoy. His mother, Olympia, née Mancini, was one of Cardinal Mazarin's nieces and a mistress of the French monarch, Louis XIV. It was Eugene's maternal grandmother, Princess Marie of Bourbon-Condé, Countess of Soissons, who dedicated herself to raising this brood. In February 1683, the young prince resolved upon a military career, intending to enter the French military service. However, he received little encouragement from his grandmother and the French king in this undertaking. So he took the path his older brother Louis-Jules (in the meantime, killed in battle) had taken before him, and turned to Emperor Leopold I, offering his services. An overwhelming Turkish army led by Kara Mustafa was threatening Vienna in 1683, inspiring Emperor Leopold I to gladly accept Eugene's services in his army. He fought in the major battle of Vienna under the command of his German cousin, Margrave Ludwig von Baden. From that time on, the brilliant military career of Prince Eugene was unstoppable. Among the early highlights numbered the conquest of Pest and Ofen, the taking of Belgrade and the victorious battle of Zenta, where Prince Eugene had the overall command. His last campaign took the Prince to the Rhineland front. He died at his palace in Vienna's inner city in 1736. During his lifetime, Prince Eugene had honours, gifts and offices lavished upon him. The most noteworthy among them was the General Governorship of the

Austrian Netherlands which he held from 1716 until 1724. This office was one of the best paid posts in the monarchy; it was generally reserved for the members of the Imperial family.

In 1697, a year after construction began on his city palace, Prince Eugene bought an appropriately large piece of land for a garden south of the Rennweg, the military road to Hungary. He immediately set out planning these gardens. His leading architect was no longer Johann Bernhard Fischer von Erlach, creator of the Winter Palace, but Johann Lucas von Hildebrandt, who had already designed Ràczkeve Castle on the island of Csepel south of Budapest for Prince Eugene, and from then onwards was responsible for carrying out all his building plans.

Johann Lucas von Hildebrandt (1668-1745) studied civil engineering in Rome with Carlo Fontana. In 1695/96 he entered the Imperial service in order to study the art of designing and building military fortifications. The architect met Prince Eugene on military campaigns in Piedmont. As of 1696, his presence is documented in Vienna as Master of Imperial Buildings. Numbering among his most outstanding works besides the Belvedere are the Schwarzenberg Palace, formerly Mansfeld-Fondi, the Daun Kinsky Palace, the Schloss Hof Palace for Prince Eugene and the entire estate of the Göttweig Monastery.

Construction of the Lower Belvedere was initiated in 1712. The work went rapidly; as early as 1715, Bolognese painter Marcantonio Chiarini was able to start his illusionistic-architectural quadrature painting in the central salon. Simultaneous with the building of the "Lustschloss" ("amusement palace"), as the Lower Belvedere was named in an artist's early city view, wide ranging garden work was also taking place.

From January to May 1717, Dominique Girard set about a complete redesigning of the gardens and completed the work the following summer. Girard, as the *fontainier du roi* in Versailles from 1707 to 1715, subsequently became Garden Inspector of Elector Emanuel of Bavaria, who recommended his services to Prince Eugene.

As early as 1717, work was begun on the Upper Belvedere. On 2 October 1719, construction had proceeded so far that Prince Eugene was able to receive the Grand Ambassador of Turkey, Ibrahim Pascha, in its halls. In 1719, Prince Eugene commissioned Neopolitan painter Francesco Solimena with both the altar paintings for the palace chapel and the ceiling paintings in the former golden room; and Gaetano Fanti with the quadrature painting of the marble salon. In 1720, Carlo Carlone was given the com-

Southern facade of Lower Belvedere, Johann Lucas von Hildebrandt

mission for the ceiling fresco in the marble salon, which he executed from 1721 to 1723. By the year 1723, the entire building was completed. During the winter of 1732/33 the Sala Terrena was given the appearance it still has today. For structural reasons - it threatened to collapse - Hildebrandt had to subsequently install a nine-arch vaulting, supported by four Atlantis figures.

Modern Gallery in the Groteskensaal of the Lower Belvedere.
Photo: Atelier Josef Löwy, 1903

Despite the fact that but little of the magnificent interior decoration of the palaces has been preserved, we can be somewhat consoled by the density of information about the original appointments of the palaces and the grounds. We have the engravings of Salomon Kleiner to thank for this. Under the title "Miraculous Wartime Victory Camp of the Unparalleled Hero of our Time, Eugenii Francisci, Duke of Savoy and Piedmont" the engineer of the Elector of Mainz completed a total of ninety plates in ten parts between 1731 and 1740 which provide a precise documentation of the palace.

Upon the death of Prince Eugene in 1736, his niece, Princess Victoria, was designated as heiress. She was the daughter of Eugene's elder brother, Thomas, and the last surviving member of the House of Savoy-Soissons. She moved into Prince Eugene's garden palace and made it clear to one and all from the outset that she had no interest whatever in her inheritance and would sell it at the earliest possible moment. In 1738 she married Prince Joseph Friedrich von Sachsen-Hildburghausen (1702-1787), several years younger than herself, but the marriage broke apart in 1744.

In 1752, Maria Theresia, daughter of Emperor Charles VI and wife of Emperor Francis Stephan of Lorraine, purchased the properties. Maria Theresia's contract to purchase the palaces that year is the first instance that the name "Belvedere" is seen in writing. As of 1776, the further elaborated names of Lower Belvedere and Upper Belvedere were used, when the Imperial art collection was moved to the two buildings. The Imperial couple never resided in the garden palace; it remained in the shadow of all the other Imperial castles and domiciles. Only in 1770 did it awaken briefly from its slumber for one single event, namely, a masqued fête on 17 April 1770 on the occasion of the wedding of the Imperial daughter Maria Antonia to the French Dauphin, the future Louis XVI. Sixteen thousand guests were invited to the festivities.

In 1776, Maria Theresia and her son, Emperor Joseph II, decided to transfer the Imperial gallery of paintings from the Stallburg, a part of the Imperial Palace in the city, to the Upper Belvedere. In the spirit of the ideals of enlightened absolutism, it was decided that the Imperial art collection should become accessible to the public. In 1781, the gallery was opened to visitors, making it one of the world's first public museums.

In the early nineteenth century, the Lower Belvedere served primarily as a domicile for Habsburg family members fleeing Napoleon. The sole surviving child of Marie Antoinette and Louis XVI, Princess Marie Thérèse Charlotte, is worth mentioning in this connection; until she married Prince Louis Antoine de Bourbon, Duke of Angoulême, in 1799, she lived in the palace. So did Maria Theresia's son, Archduke Ferdinand, who was Captain General of Lombardy until 1796, when he was forced to hand over his lands to the French under the terms of the Peace of Campo Formio (1797), leaving him without a residence.

After Tyrol was ceded to Bavaria at the Peace of Pressburg in 1805, a new location for the Imperial collections at Ambras Castle near Innsbruck had to be found. From 1811, following an edict of Emperor Francis I, they were housed in the Lower Belvedere. As of the year 1833, the collection of Egyptian treasures and the ancient cabinet of the Ambras collection were also added to the Lower Belvedere. This situation remained nearly unchanged until the Imperial collections were ultimately transferred to the newly built Kunsthistorisches Museum on the Ring Road in the heart of Vienna in 1888/89.

After the Imperial collections were removed, the two Belvedere palaces ceased to be publicly accessible museums and had to be assigned a new purpose. In 1896, Emperor Franz Joseph I decided to make the Upper Belvedere a residence for the heir apparent, his nephew Franz Ferdinand. The upper palace was subsequently rebuilt into a residence for Franz Ferdinand and served as his domicile from then on.

In the Lower Belvedere, the "Modern Gallery" opened its portals on 2 May 1903. This museum was conceived as Austria's first national collection of art works dedicated exclusively to the modern era. It can be attributed to the initiative of the Association of Graphic Artists in Austria ("Vereinigung Bildender Künstler Österreichs"), usually known by the name of the Secession. It was their objective to exhibit local contemporary art next to international modern art works. Thus, at the beginning of the "Modern Gallery" era, major works by Van Gogh, Monet and Segantini were purchased and displayed. This concentration on modern art works was soon expanded, following the decision that works of earlier epochs should also be purchased. In this spirit, the museum was rechristened as the "Imperial State Gallery" ("k.und k. Staatsgalerie") in 1911.

Following the murder of the heir apparent and his wife in 1914, the Upper Belvedere no longer served any clearly defined purpose, so it was utilized as a museum. The collection of art from the nineteenth century was housed here. In particular, the art of Vienna's Biedermeier period, including works by Ferdinand Georg Waldmüller, became a focal point. In the Lower Belvedere, a new Baroque museum with works from the 17th and 18th centuries was established, in which the famous character portraits by Franz Xaver Messerschmidt stand out. In the so-called Orangerie, the art of the twentieth century was on view, including works by artists such as Gustav Klimt and Egon Schiele.

The Second World War caused heavy damages to the substance of the palace buildings, and the collections had to be closed. After the buildings were finally restored, the museum was reopened in 1953. It was now named the "Österreichische Galerie". In the Orangerie, the collection of medieval Austrian art, including works from the 13th through 16th centuries, was established. The following years brought many new additions to the collection, particularly of Austrian art.

In 1978, the erstwhile atelier of sculptor Gustinus Ambrosi in the Augarten (2nd Vienna district) was purchased by the Belvedere. A bevy of sculptures by this artist who died in 1975 have since found their home in a museum devoted to them. After a comprehensive renovation of the atelier in the year 2000, an additional exhibition room was created. Under the name of "augarten contemporary", it sponsors changing exhibitions devoted to the works of young contemporary artists.

In 2002, the "20er Haus" - concentrating on the works of the twentieth century - was established in the Österreichische Galerie. This building was the headquarters of the Museum of the 20th Century, founded in 1962, which ceased to have a function after the collection was transferred to the Museum of Modern Art, Ludwig Foundation, in the new Museum District. The former exhibition pavilion, built by Austrian architect Karl Schwanzer (1918-1975) for the Great Exhibition of 1958 in Brussels, is a major work of Austria's post-World War II functional architecture. As of the year 2010, after major renovations and adaptations by the architectural bureau of Adolf Krischanitz, it will house the post-1945 collection of art of the Belvedere.

20er Haus, external view, Karl Schwanzer (1918-1975)

In 2007-2008, the Baroque and Medieval art collections, which until then had been housed in the Lower Belvedere and in the Orangerie, were transferred to the Upper Belvedere. The Lower Belvedere and the Orangerie were given over to wide ranging reconstruction and adaptation of the original buildings. They now house changing exhibitions. In the so-called Grand Stables, the former housing for Prince Eugene's own horses, the "Medieval Treasure House" was established. In the form of storage/exhibition rooms, the remaining works of medieval art, which until then had simply been stored in the depot rooms, have been made accessible to the public. Thus, all the sectors of the various collections, from the Middle Ages to the twentieth century, are now on view in the Upper Belvedere, providing museum visitors with an incomparable and comprehensive experience of art.

MIDDLE AGES

The medieval collection is one of the younger domains which the Belvedere has assembled, comprising about 220 works from the Romanesque to High Gothic periods. The focus is on sculptures and altar panels of the 14th to early 16th centuries, providing a representative overview both of the evolution and the immense diversity of Gothic art in Austria. Among the important early sculptures are the highly expressive Madonna by Sonntagberger and the group of figures by the Master of Grosslobming, from the period of stylistic beauty around 1400, distinguished by superb gracefulness, soft, flowing robes and a subtle if superficial sensuality. The fundamental transformation towards early realism is documented in imposing fashion by the Viennese Albrechtsmeister and the Znaimer Altar, whose bas-reliefs of the Agony of Christ still manifest the original, detailed painting of the sculpture. The major works of the subsequent generations are from Conrad Laib, master painter of the Viennese Schotten Altar, Rueland Frueauf the elder and the younger, Michael Pacher, Marx Reichlich, Hans Klocker, Urban Görtschacher and numerous other masters, often not known by name, from various regions.

Only very few Gothic panels in today's collection were part of the original collection of the Imperial Art Gallery at the Upper Belvedere of 1781. After transferring the Habsburg art treasures to the Kunsthistorische Imperial Museum, which first opened its portals in 1891, the Belvedere was assigned the role, stage by stage, of becoming an Austrian "National Museum": the Modern Gallery, built into the Lower Belvedere in 1903, was rededicated as the Imperial Staatsgalerie in 1911 by Friedrich Dörnhöffer. It was intended to include all art epochs, including the Middle Ages. When the monarchy came to an end, the Republic of Austria took possession of the imperial art collections and authorized their reorganisation by the Vienna Museum Programme of 1920/21. To begin with, only Hans Tietze and Alfred Stix's plan for establishing an Austrian Baroque museum was realized. For that reason, the objects intended to be the basis of a medieval collection were transferred to the Kunsthistorische Museum, where this collection was greatly enlarged by important acquisitions in the early 1920's. It was not until after World War Two that museum director Karl Garzarolli-Thurnlakh, himself a medievalist deeply devoted to building an inventory of art from the Middle Ages at the Belvedere, succeeded in retrieving a large part of these works back from the Kunsthistorische Museum in exchange for others. Finally, on 5 December 1953, the Museum of Medieval Austrian Art was opened in the Orangerie.

In 2007, the collection was newly structured. At the Upper Belvedere, there are now about 60 Gothic masterpieces on exhibit. All the other altars, panels and sculptures can be viewed in the newly furbished showrooms known as "Treasure House Middle Ages" in Prince Eugene's Grand Stables at the Lower Belvedere. Thus, for the first time in the history of this building, profound insight into one of the most important medieval art collections of Central Europe is provided.

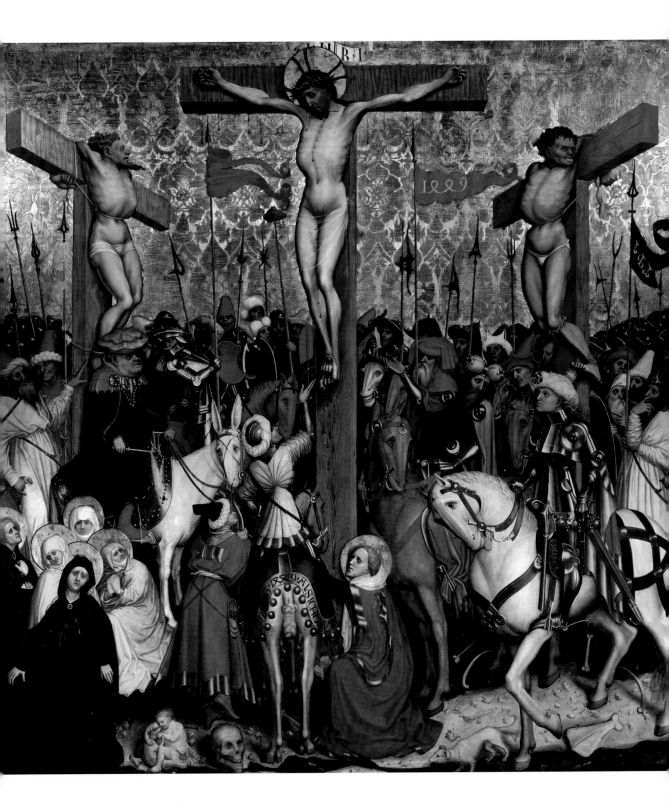

Conrad LAIB
Crucifixion of Christ, 1449
painting on pinewood
179x179 cm
signed on the banner "1449" on horse blanket of rider in front
of the cross "D PFENNING. 1449. ALSICH CHUN"
Belvedere, Vienna. Inv.Nr.4919

SALZBURG PAINTER (?)
Birth of Christ, around 1400
painting on beechwood
41 x 29,5 cm
Belvedere, Vienna, Inv.-Nr. 4894

MASTER OF HEILIGENKREUZ
Mystical marriage of St. Catharine, around 1415/1420
painting on oakwood (?)
21,5 x 18,5 cm
Belvedere, Vienna, Inv.-Nr. 9239

STYRIAN CARVER (?)
Virgin Mary on lunar arc
around 1430
limewood, painted,
details gilded,
height: 101 cm
Belvedere, Vienna, Inv.-Nr. 6152

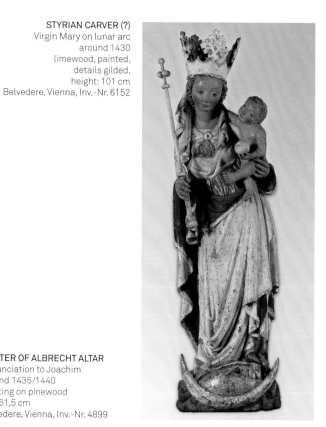

MASTER OF ALBRECHT ALTAR
Annunciation to Joachim
around 1435/1440
painting on pinewood
96 x 61,5 cm
Belvedere, Vienna, Inv.-Nr. 4899

TYROLEAN CARVER
Crucifixion, late 12th century/around 1200
alderwood, residue of painted form, cross not original
corpus: 88,5 x 78 cm
overall: 103 x 97 cm
Belvedere, Vienna, Inv.-Nr. 5986

MICHAELER MASTER
Madonna of Mt. Sunday, around 1360
poplarwood, original undercoat
height: 184 cm
standing surface area: 48x36 cm
Belvedere, Vienna, Inv.-Nr. 4831

MASTER OF GROSSLOBMING
Kneeling Angel of Annunciation Group
late 14th century
Breitenbrunn limestone, original residue of painted form
height: 78 cm
standing surface area: : 45,5 x 25,5 cm
Belvedere, Vienna, Inv.-Nr. 4901

11

MASTER OF FRIEDRICH ALTAR (workshop)
VIENNESE CARVER AND SCULPTURE PAINTER
Znaimer Altar, around 1440/1450
Limewood reliefs on pinewood boards, original oakwood frame, largely original painting, gold background of right panel renewed around 1500,
painting on pinewood on outer side of panels
Overall: 255 x 522 cm
Shrine: 255 x 174 cm
Panels: 255 x 124 cm
Belvedere, Vienna, Inv.-Nr. 4847

MASTER OF SCHOTTEN ALTAR
Lamentation of Christ, around 1470
Oil painting on oakwood
87 x 80 cm

Belvedere, Vienna, Inv.-Nr. 4854

MASTER OF SCHOTTEN ALTAR
Worship of Three Holy Kings, around 1470
Oil painting on oakwood
86 x 80 cm
Belvedere, Vienna, Inv.-Nr. 4855

Michael PACHER
Pope Sixtus II's farewell to St. Lawrence, around 1465
Painting on stone pine
104 x 100 cm
Belvedere, Vienna, Inv.-Nr. 4836

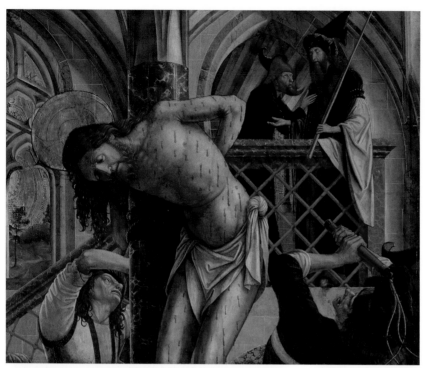

Michael PACHER
Flagellation of Christ
before 1497/1498
Painting on stone pine
113 x 139,5 cm
Belvedere, Vienna, Inv.-Nr. 4845

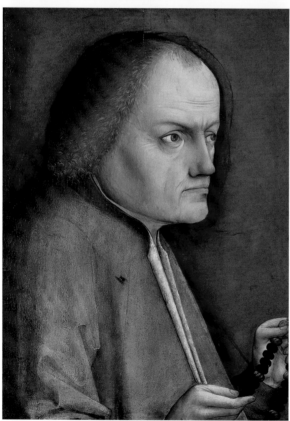

Ludwig KONRAITER (?)
INNSBRUCK COURT PAINTER
Portrait of Sigismund "Rich in Coin", Archduke of Tyrol,
around 1480/1490
Painting on pinewood
42,5 x 33,5 cm
Belvedere, Vienna, Inv.-Nr. 4890

Rueland FRUELAUF THE ELDER
Portrait of a Young Man (Jobst Seyfried?), around 1495
Painting on limewood
25x18.3 cm
signed at top center "R.F.", signed on reverse side with name of
person portrayed or of owner (?): "W/ENAE/IOBST/SEIFRID"
Belvedere, Vienna, Inv.-Nr. 4828

Marx REICHLICH
The Visitation, 1502 (?)
Painting on pinewood
66,5 x 77 cm
Belvedere, Vienna, Inv.-Nr. 4879

Hans KLOCKER
Virgin Mary in a praying group
around 1485/1490
Sculpted of stone pine,
painted and gilded
height: 114 cm
Belvedere, Vienna, Inv.-Nr. 4985a

Hans KLOCKER
St. Joseph in a
praying group
around 1485/1490
Sculpted of stone
pine, painted
116 x 53 x 40 cm
Belvedere, Vienna,
Inv.-Nr. 7467

Rueland FRUELAUF THE ELDER
Assumption of Virgin Mary, 1490
Painting on pinewood, framework renewed (2007)
209x134 cm
signed and dated on tombstone "R.F.1490"

Belvedere, Vienna, Inv.-Nr. 4844

MASTER OF LAKE MONDSEE
Flight to Egypt, before 1499
Painting on firwood
57,5 x 45 cm
Belvedere, Vienna, Inv.-Nr. 4827

BAROQUE

The history of the Baroque collection at the Belvedere is closely associated with the art collecting activities of the original builder of the Belvedere palaces, Prince Eugene of Savoy. The epicentre of this collection of paintings was the "Painting Salon" or Gallery of the Upper Belvedere. This gallery comprised mostly Italian and Dutch masters. Individual paintings of this original collection, such as paintings by Johann Georg de Hamilton or Franz Werner Tamm, are still part of the Belvedere collection today. Following the establishment of the "Austrian Gallery", a new Baroque museum was established in the Lower Belvedere including major masters of Austrian Baroque art of the 17th and 18th centuries. In 2008, this collection was reexhibited effectively in a concentrated new presentation in the Upper Belvedere.

Within the collection at the Belvedere, the most prominent themes can be pinpointed. For example, court portraits by international virtuosos such as Jacob van Schuppen and Martin van Meytens are present, which depict the social status and the appropriate poses and insignias corresponding to that status, as symbols of power at the zenith of absolutism. Nearly at the same time, a completely different movement developed, namely of the personal sphere underscored by the works of Jan Kupetzky, Christian Seybold and Franz Anton Palko. The still lifes and the festive culture of the Baroque era might best be summarised by the motto "loud and serene life". Festivities in the inner chambers of the palaces and in the extensive gardens, often staged with Baroque theater, music and dance performances, are revealed in the phantastic, secretly sensuous worlds of painters such as Johann Georg Platzer and Franz Christoph Janneck. The painting of still lifes is at least as refined in degree. It contains scientifically inspired, small scale works of Johann Adalbert Angermayer or Franz Michael Siegmund of Purgau, for example. The quiet world of magical corporeality becomes palpable in the compass-designed kitchen still lifes of Anna Maria Punz.

The series of works of the so-called "character heads" by Franz Xaver Messerschmidt dazzle the viewer through their aggressiveness and modernity in the positive sense of radical human portrayal. In these experiments in physical mimicry which produce extreme contortions, a certain stimulus from Lavater's "Physiognomic Fragments" (via the teachings of Lichtenberg and those of Franz Anton Mesmer, magnetiseur and miracle healer) can be assumed. The Belvedere owns the world's largest collection of busts which are designated by the artist as "Portraits," admittedly an oversimplification.

Important examples of religious and mythological historical painting can be seen in the works of Johann Michael Rottmayr, Martino Altomonte, Paul Troger, Franz Anton Maulbertsch and Kremser Schmidt. In the Baroque era, these works were created for churches, monasteries and palaces, and were assigned the very highest rank in the entire discipline of painting. Landscape painting in the second half of the eighteenth century is distinguished by the work of Johann Christian Brand, who in the so-called "Reiherbeize" in Laxenburg Castle, created a realistic depiction of the hilly landscape surrounding Vienna.

Johann Michael ROTTMAYR
Lamentation of Abel, 1692
Oil painting on linen
191x127 cm
signed lower right: "Jo. Michael Rotmayr Fecit 1692"
Belvedere, Vienna, Inv.-Nr. 4298

Franz Werner TAMM
Domestic fowl and rabbit, around 1706
Oil painting on linen
137x186 cm
unsigned
Belvedere, Vienna, Inv.-Nr. 4148

Martino ALTOMONTE
Susanna and the two old men, 1709
Oil painting on linen
131x107 cm
lower right: "Mar... Altomonte Fecit 1709"
Belvedere, Vienna, Inv.-Nr. 4243

Jan KUPETZKY
Self-portrait at the easel, 1709
Oil painting on linen
94x75 cm
lower left: Iohan. Kuprzky Pinxit. 1709
Belvedere, Vienna, Inv.-Nr. 4939

Franz Anton PALKO
Self-portrait, 1746
Oil on copper
42-32 cm
lower right: F. Anton Palcko Pinxit.1746
Belvedere, Vienna, Inv.-Nr. 7645

Johann Gottfried AUERBACH
Prince Eugene of Savoy
(1663-1736), before 1723 (?)
Oil painting on linen
201x138 cm
unsigned
Belvedere, Vienna, Inv.-Nr. Lg 200

Jacob van SCHUPPEN
Prince Eugene of Savoy
(1663-1736), after 1717
Oil painting on linen
130x150 cm
unsigned
Belvedere, Vienna, Inv.-Nr. Lg 1140

Johann Georg PLATZER
Rebecca at the fountain,
around 1740
Oil on copper
37.5x49.5 cm
unsigned
Belvedere, Vienna, Inv.-Nr. 8521

Franz Christoph JANNECK
Outdoor gathering
The Dance, around 1740
Oil painted on wood
41-62 cm
lower right: F. C. Janneck fec
Belvedere, Vienna, Inv.-Nr. 4179

Balthasar PERMOSER
The Apotheosis of
Prince Eugene of Savoy
(1663-1736), 1718-1721
white marble
height: 230cm
pedestal inscription
(in metallic lettering):
F(RANCISCUS) EUGENIUS.SABAUD(IAE)
ET.PEDEMONT(IS).PRINCEPS.MARCHIO.
SALUT(IENSIUM).AUR(EI).VELL(ERIS).
EQUES.CAROLI.VI.AUG(USTI).ET.S(ACRI)
R(OMANI). I(MPERII).SUPREMUS.
EXERCITUUM.DUX.INVICTISSIMUS.
Belvedere, Vienna, Inv.-Nr. 4219

Christian Hilfgott BRAND
Landscape with pedestal, 1753
Oil on wood
40x48 cm
lower right: Brand 1753
Belvedere, Vienna, Inv.-Nr. 4087

Franz Anton MAULPERTSCH
Erecting the cross,around 1750-1755
Oil painting on linen
147x113 cm
lower center: Maulbertsch. adjacent: Distel
Belvedere, Vienna, Inv.-Nr. 3289

Franz Xaver MESSERSCHMIDT
Maria Theresia (1717-1780)
as Queen of Hungary
(1740-1780), around 1765
tin-copper alloy
height: 202 cm
lower left: F.M.SH:
Belvedere, Vienna, Inv.-Nr. 2239

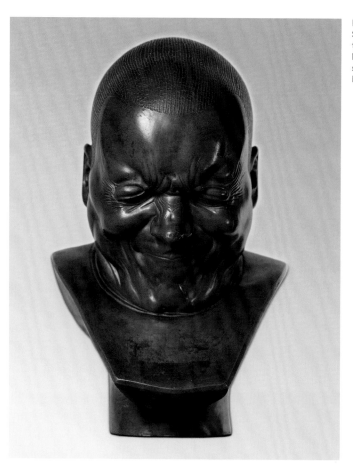

Franz Xaver MESSERSCHMIDT
Striking head: "An Arch-Villain", after 1770
tin-lead alloy
height 38.5 cm
stamped lower left in base: 33
Belvedere, Vienna, Inv.-Nr. 2442

Franz Xaver MESSERSCHMIDT
Striking head: "A Hanged Man", after 1770
alabaster plaster
height: 38 cm
unsigned
Belvedere, Vienna, Inv.-Nr. 5637

Franz Xaver MESSERSCHMIDT
Striking head
"Second strong-beaked man", after 1770
alabaster plaster
height: 43 cm
unsigned
Belvedere, Vienna, Inv.-Nr. 5640

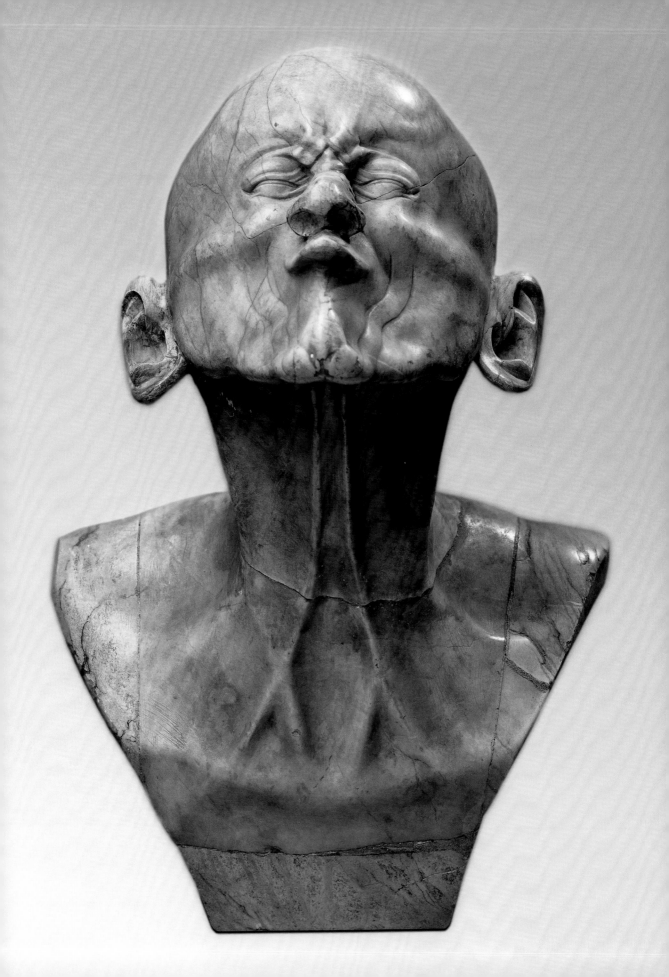

CLASSICISM

Antique pictures unearthed and studied in Rome and Pompei ever since the mid eighteenth century were the guiding light of Classicism, which rose in importance to become the dominant style in Europe at the end of the 18th century. The artistic expressiveness of this epoch leans heavily on works and culture of ancient Greece and Rome.

The teachings of the Enlightenment, including a demand for individualisation of all human beings, also left clear and palpable traces in the art around 1800. Soon after the middle of the 1700's, outstanding portraits were being produced all over Europe, but particularly in Vienna, whose artists strived towards an utterly new mode of human portrayal. The shining example for Austrian painters was English portrait painting. A vivid illustration of this is the portrait "John Simpson, Father of Maria Susanna Lady Ravensworth", which Vorarlberg artist Angelika Kauffmann painted during her long sojourn in London. Yet the most interesting portraits of this era were doubtless by Josef Kreutzinger, a nearly unknown painter today. He borrowed heavily from his English role models, as did Friedrich Heinrich Füger, the Academy's famous director. This English influence can also be seen in the depiction of a person's psychological state as evidenced by posture and bearing as well as in the fluid painting technique and the broad, swift brushstrokes.

France figured prominently in setting both tone and taste for European portrait painting. During a sojourn in France, the Viennese Count, Moritz Christian Fries, commissioned the most illustrious portrait painter of the era, François Gérard, to fashion a painting of him together with his wife and very young child. The painting, which later on found its way to the Belvedere, boasts a smooth surface, an imposing trueness of detail and a meticulously precise execution. The grand master of French Classicism, Jacues Louis David, is also represented at the Belvedere with his splendid 1801 work, the large scale painting "Napoleon on the St. Bernard Pass". As Napoleon's court painter, Jacques Louis David created a commemorative picture of the military campaign on which the First Consul embarked over the Great St. Bernard in 1800 before descending to occupy Lombardy. Paintings such as these evidence a brand new approach to historical painting, which simultaneously transferred the focus to current political events.

The group of mythological figures in the painting "Mars and Venus with Cupid" by Leopold Kiesling, who was residing in Rome on a stipend, also lends itself to interpretation in dynastic-political ways. This patriotic allegory in marble was completed in 1809, the very year of Napoleon and Archduchess Marie Louise of Austria's wedding. Emperor Francis I., father of Marie Louise, had commissioned this sculpture at a time when the dynastic connection between Austria and France was not a subject of dispute, however. With similar inspiration, the bust of "Empress Maria Ludovica", which Johann Nepomuk Schaller completed a short time later, also takes its inspiration from historical ideals.

Friedrich Heinrich FÜGER
Empress Maria Theresia (1740-1780) encircled by her children, 1776
tempera on parchment
34.2x39 cm
signed at base: "H. F. Füger pinx: 1776"
Belvedere, Vienna, Inv.-Nr. 2296

Angelika KAUFFMANN
John Simpson, father of Maria
Susanna Lady Ravensworth, 1773
Oil painting on linen
127x101.5 cm
signed on right side: "Angelika Kauffman/pinx 1773"
Belvedere, Vienna, Inv.-Nr. 8504

Friedrich Heinrich FÜGER
Actress Josepha Hortensia Füger, née Müller (1766-1807),
wife of the artist, around 1797
Oil painting on linen
113x88.5 cm
unsigned
Belvedere, Vienna, Inv.-Nr. 4194

Josef Kreutzinger
Karl Ferdinand, Count Kinsky (?) in the uniform of an honourary
knight of the sovereign Maltese Order, around 1790
Oil painting on linen
81.5x63 cm
unsigned
Belvedere, Vienna, Inv.-Nr. Lg 53

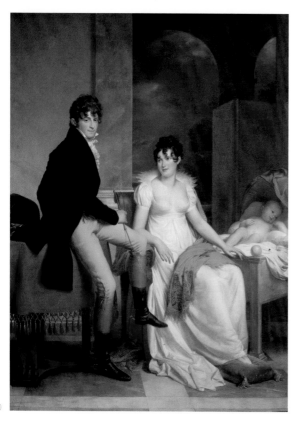

François Pascal Simon GÉRARD
Count Moritz Christian Fries and his family,
around 1804
Oil painting on linen
233x163.5 cm
signed lower left: "F. GÉRARD"
Belvedere, Vienna, Inv.-Nr. 3386

Vinzenz FISCHER
Allegory of Transfer of Imperial Gallery to Belvedere, 1781
Oil painting on linen
57x47 cm
signed lower right: 13 OK 1781 V.Fischer
Belvedere, Vienna, Inv.-Nr. 4229

31

Leopold KIESLING
Mars and Venus with Cupid, 1809
Carrara marble
height: 222 cm
signed on base: "LEOP.KISSLING:FECIT."
ROMA MDCCCVIIII"
Belvedere, Vienna, Inv.-Nr. 2555

Johann Nepomuk SCHALLER
Empress Maria Ludovica Beatrix (1787-1816),
Third wife of Emperor Franz II's (I) of Austria (1792-1835), 1814
Carrara marble on base of stucco marble
height 61 cm; inc. base: 71 cm
signed on rear side at base: "JOHANN SCHALLER ROM 1814"
Belvedere, Vienna, Inv.-Nr. 2289

Jacques Louis DAVID
Napoleon on the St. Bernard Pass, 1801
Oil painting on linen
246x231 cm
signed on horse's harness: "J.L.DAVID.F.ANNOX.REI.C",
signed lower left: "BONOPARTE / HANNIBAL / CAROLUS
MAGNUS MP" (intertwined)
Belvedere, Vienna, Inv.-Nr. 2089

BIEDERMEIER ROMANTICISM

The Belvedere has the nation's largest collection of works from Vienna's Biedermeier era. Biedermeier is the term used to characterize the epoch between the Congress of Vienna in 1814/15 and the Revolution of 1848. After the French Revolution of 1789, the middle class played a major role in the political and cultural life of society. Art commissions were no longer granted only by the ruling dynasty, the nobility and the Church, but also by properous bourgeois families. A dynamic art market evolved at the exhibitions of the art academies and associations. This new clientele was also well suited to the format of the paintings, since the Biedermeier era paintings were usually small.

In the works of Biedermeier painters, the private sphere of the citizens became one of the central themes. Portraits of family members, such as in the large painting "Rudolf von Arthaber with his Children" by Friedrich von Amerling, soon were an indispensable part of every self-respecting bourgeois household. The depictions do not even draw the line at the intimate living sphere of the citizens. The depictions of reading or sleeping people, as in the painting "Reading Girl" by Franz Eybl or Johann Baptist Reiter's painting "Woman Dozing" are quite amusing examples of this trend. Ferdinand Georg Waldmüller, on the other hand, takes up the role of pictorial chronicler of the rural population, as his paintings "On the Morning of the Feast of Corpus Christi" or "The Brushwood Collector" vividly illustrate. Another hallmark of these realisitic depictions was their moralizing component, at least in many cases. To this end, "The Splurging Rich Man" by Josef Danhauser was intended to stir the population to increase their spirit of charitable giving, or the painting "Girl Before the Lotto" by Peter Fendi aimed to warn of the dangers of gambling.

In each genre that Viennese painters took up during the early decades of the nineteenth century, a preference for realism can be seen. This is evident not only in the scientific precision of flower paintings and still lifes, but also in the landscapes which are so true to reality. Artists such as Josef Rebell, Ferdinand Georg Waldmüller, Franz Steinfeld, Friedrich Gauermann, Thomas Ender and Rudolf von Alt are all pioneers of the realistic depiction of nature. For example, the painting "Bernese Oberland" numbers among the major works of early landscape paintings by Tyrolean artist Josef Anton Koch, as does "The Broad Pine at Brühl Valley near Mödling" by artist Ludwig Ferdinand Schnorr von Carolsfeld, who stemmed from Königsberg and lived in Vienna.

Comparisons of Austrian painters with German artists, for example Carl Blechen's "Afternoon on Capri", illustrate in graphic ways their divergent approaches. They differ equally from a romantic approach to nature depiction enriched by symbolism, as represented by German artist Caspar David Friedrich, many of whose important works are on view in the Belvedere collection.

Religious painting in the Biedermeier era is influenced both in content and in style by the Lukasbund Association, founded in Vienna in 1809. After the appearance of this group, painters became known as "Nazarenes". One major work in this style is the painting "The Three Holy Kings" by Leopold Kupelwieser.

Caspar David FRIEDRICH
Seashore with fisherman, around 1807
Oil painting on linen
33.5x51 cm
unsigned
Belvedere, Vienna, Inv.-Nr. 3701

Joseph REBELL
Sea storm at Arco di Miseno near Miliscola
with view towards Nisida, 1819
Oil painting on linen
99x137 cm
signed lower left: "Jos. Rebell 1819"
Belvedere, Vienna, Inv.-Nr. 2123

Josef Anton KOCH
Bernese Oberland, 1815
Oil painting on linen
70x89 cm
signed lower left: "GIUSEPPE KOCH /
TYROLESE / FECE 1815"
Belvedere, Vienna, Inv.-Nr. 2622

Johann KNAPP
Jacquin's Memorial, 1821-1822
Oil painting on linen
218x164 cm
signed lower right on stone base: "JOHANN KNAPP /
FECIT / MDCCCXXII / SCHOENBRUNN",
on marble pedestal: "VOCAT NATURA / ARTEM /
UTRAQUE / TE IMMORTALEM./ OPST MEYER.",
signed on right side: "LINNAEI."
Belvedere, Vienna, Inv.-Nr. 3651

Caspar David FRIEDRICH
View of the Elbe (left window) from artist's studio in
Dresden, around 1805-1806
sepia on paper
31.4x23.5 cm
On the letter in the window the address can be read:
"to Mr. C. D. Friedrich in Dresden, at the Pirnasch
Gate." Belvedere, Vienna, Inv.-Nr. 1850

Friedrich August Mathias GAUERMANN
Lake Altaussee with Dachstein, around 1827
Oil painting on paper on linen
30x43 cm
signed lower left: "AltAussee / von Friedrich Gauermann"
Belvedere, Vienna, Inv.-Nr. Lg 50

Carl BLECHEN
Afternoon on Capri, around 1829
Oil painting on linen
91-130 cm
unsigned
Belvedere, Vienna, Inv.-Nr. 1996

Caspar David FRIEDRICH
Rocky landscape in Elb
Sandstone Massif
around 1822-1823
Oil painting on linen
94x74 cm
unsigned
Belvedere, Vienna, Inv.-Nr. 2589

Michael Johann NEDER
Coachmen's dispute, 1828
Oil painting on linen
58x71 cm
signed lower left: Neder pinxit
/ 1828
Belvedere, Vienna, Inv.-Nr. 4392

Leopold KUPELWIESER
The Three Holy Kings, 1825
Oil painted on wood
33x41.5 cm
signed lower left: "Kupelwieser./
1825."
Belvedere, Vienna, Inv.-Nr. 3768

Josef DANHAUSER
The Scholars' Room, 1828
Oil painting on linen
43.5x51.5 cm
lower left, illegible remains of a signature.
Belvedere, Vienna, Inv.-Nr. 2109

Peter FENDI
Maiden at the lottery vault
Oil painting on linen
63-50 cm
signed lower left: "Fendi p./1829."
Belvedere, Vienna, Inv.-Nr. 2177

Josef DANHAUSER
The Rich Man Splurges, 1836
Oil painting on linen
84x131 cm
signed lower right on doorpost:
"Danhauser Vienna 1936"
Belvedere, Vienna, Inv.-Nr. 2087

Josef NIGG
Floral bouquet, around 1835
Oil painting on linen
79.7x63.3 cm
signed lower right: "Jos: Nigg."
Belvedere, Vienna, Inv.-Nr. 3630

Ferdinand Georg WALDMÜLLER
Self-portrait as a young man, 1828
Oil painting on linen
95,2 x 75,2 cm
signed lower left: „Waldmüller 1828 Aet. 35"
Belvedere, Vienna, Inv.-Nr. 2121

Ludwig Ferdinand SCHNORR VON CAROLSFELD
Broad Pine in the Brühl near Mödling,, 1838
Oil painting on linen
66x112
signed lower left: "18 LS 38" (L and S
intertwined)
Belvedere, Vienna, Inv.-Nr. 3167

Franz STEINFELD THE YOUNGER
Lake Hallstätter, 1834
Oil painting on linen
57x48 cm
signed lower right: Steinfeld / 1834
Belvedere, Vienna, Inv.-Nr. 5023

Ferdinand Georg WALDMÜLLER
Roses in a glass, 1831
Oil painted on wood
30.5x26 cm
signed lower center: "Waldmüller 1831"
Belvedere, Vienna, Inv.-Nr. 2332

Friedrich von AMERLING
Rudolf von Arthaber (1795-1867) with his
children Rudolf, Emilie and Gustav, gazing at
the portrait of his deceased mother, Johanna
Georgine Karoline,née von Scheidlin (1833)
1837
Oil painting on linen
221-155 cm
signed lower right: "Fr. Amerling /†1837"
Belvedere, Vienna, Inv.-Nr. 2245

Friedrich von AMERLING
The Lute Player, 1838
Oil painting on linen
99x82 cm
signed on left side: "Fr Amerling / 1838"
Belvedere, Vienna, Inv.-Nr. Lg 40

Ferdinand Georg WALDMÜLLER
Still life with fruits, flowers and silver trophy,
1839
Oil painted on wood
signed on left side: "Waldmüller 1839"
Belvedere, Vienna, Inv.-Nr. 876

Rudolf von ALT
St. Stephan's Cathedral in Vienna, 1832 (detail)
Oil painting on linen
46x57.5 cm
signed at lower left: "Rudolph Alt 1832"
Belvedere, Vienna, Inv.-Nr. 2081

Johann Baptist REITER
Slumbering woman, 1849
Oil painted on wood
56x69 cm
signed lower right: "J. B: Reiter Vienna / 849"
48   Belvedere, Vienna, Inv.-Nr. 5547

Franz EYBL
Maiden reading
Oil painting on linen
53x41 cm
signed at lower left: "F.EIBL./1850"
Belvedere, Vienna, Inv.-Nr. 7333

Thomas ENDER
Grossglockner with Pasterze Glacier, 1832
Oil painting on linen
39x54 cm
signed lower right: "Thom. Ender.nach der Natur 1832"
Belvedere, Vienna, Inv.-Nr. 6068

Ferdinand Georg WALDMÜLLER
On Corpus Christi Morning, 1857 (detail)
Oil painted on wood
65x82 cm
signed left center: "Waldmüller 1857"
Belvedere, Vienna, Inv.-Nr. Lg 63

IMPRESSIONISM

In the nineteenth century, landscapes played an important part in the development of modern painting. One of the earliest groups of artists that devoted itself to painting outdoors in nature was the Barbizon School, who formed near Paris as of about 1830. Gustave Courbet, grand master of French realism, was in close contact with this group. Camille Corot is also present in the wider membership of this school; he demonstrates intense atmospheric feeling in his small sized 1843 work "Lake Nemi". Jean-Francois Millet joined this tradition as well.

The Barbizon School laid the foundations for Impressionism. The paintings of the Impressionists attained a luminosity never before been achieved. The landscape motifs are often composed of loosely applied splashes of pigment, awakening an impression of great spontaneousness. Through his landscape paintings, Claude Monet is the undisputed icon of Impressionism. Portraits, however, came seldom from his hand. The Belvedere collection has one of the rare portraits by Claude Monet, namely, "The Chef (Monsieur Paul)" from 1882. The work was purchased at the famous Impressionist exhibition in the Viennese Secession in 1903. Monet's 1902 painting "Path in Monet's Garden" is, on the other hand, a magnificent work from the series of paintings of the artist's garden in Giverny. Whereas Monet and Camille Pissarro devoted themselves primarily to landscapes, Eduard Manet, August Renoir and Edgar Degas preferred spontaneous renderings of human figures. Renoir's 1903 painting "Bathing Woman with Long Blonde Hair" is one of the typical examples of the sensual melding of colours in a woman's naked body.

Impressionist paintings awakened great interest in Austria as well. The Viennese painter Carl Schuch was initially a member of Munich's renowned Leibl Circle, before he joined the ranks of painters who discovered painting outdoors in nature. His works painted in the Vienna Woods, such as "Forest Clearing near Pukersdorf" from 1872, succeeded astonishingly well in a creation of impressionistic effects. Simultaneously, a circle of students formed around artist Emil Jakob Schindler. Schindler's landscape paintings are characterized by a profound immersion into depicting the atmosphere surrounding thunderstorms, such as can be seen in the 1884 painting "Atmosphere of February (Pre-Spring in the Vienna Woods)". Schindler, together with Tina Blau-Lang, Olga Wisinger-Florian and Theodor von Hörmann, cultivated the so-called Impressionism of Atmosphere, a poetic variation of Impressionistic landscape painting. Carl Moll must also be counted in this circle through his early works, as the 1894 painting "The Naschmarkt in Vienna" makes amply clear.

In Germany, painters Max Liebermann, Max Slevogt and Lovis Corinth are among the most important German Impressionists. The Belvedere collection has important works by all three artists, for example, Liebermann's 1913 painting "Hunter in the Dunes". The particular candour and dynamics of the brushstrokes of his paintings attain a high intensity, which then, in the paintings of Lovis Corinth, crosses over the threshold to Expressionism.

Camille COROT
Lake Nemi, 1843
Oil painting on linen
23.2x29.8 cm
signed lower right: "VENTE / COROT",
on reverse side on frame (seal): "VENTE
COROT"
Belvedere, Vienna, Inv.-Nr. 3149

Camille COROT
Madame Legois, around 1840-1845
Oil painting on linen
55x40 cm
signed on left side: "COROT"
Belvedere, Vienna, Inv.-Nr. 2413

August von PETTENKOFEN
Transporting the Wounded i, 1853
Oil painted on cardboard
26.5x35 cm
lower left: A.Pettenkofen 1853
Belvedere, Vienna, Inv.-Nr. 6000

Honoré DAUMIER
Sancho Panza, resting against a tree, around 1860
Oil painting on linen
100x81.5 cm
signed lower right: "h.D."
Belvedere, Vienna, Inv.-Nr. 1056

Jean-François MILLET
The Chailly Plain with plow
and harrow, 1862
Oil painting on linen
60.3x73.6 cm
signed lower right: "J.F.MILLET"
Belvedere, Vienna, Inv.-Nr. 2450

Gustave COURBET
Wounded Man, around 1866
Oil painting on linen
79.5x99.5 cm
signed lower left: "G. Courbet"
Belvedere, Vienna, Inv.-Nr. 2376

Carl SCHUCH
Forest clearing near Purkersdorf, around 1872
Oil painted on cardboard
53.5x41 cm
unsigned
Belvedere, Vienna, Inv.-Nr. 1251

Camille Jacob PISSARRO
Street in Pontoise (Rue de Gisors), 1868
Oil painting on linen
38.5x46.2 cm
signed lower left: "C.Pissarro 1868"
Belvedere, Vienna, Inv.-Nr. 1281

Emil Jakob SCHINDLER
Steamboat station on the Danube
across from Kaisermühlen, around 1871-1872
Oil painting on linen
55x78.5 cm
signed lower left: "Naturstudie aus dem Prater /
gemalt und seinem
Freund Dr. J. Scholz {…} gewidmet von E.J.Schindler"
Belvedere, Vienna, Inv.-Nr. 3338

Edouard MANET
Lady in fur, around 1880
Pastel painted on linen
55.8x45.8 cm
signed right center: "Manet"
Belvedere, Vienna, Inv.-Nr. 3867

Edgar DEGAS
Harlequin and Colombine, around 1886
Pastel on paper
42.8x42.8 cm
signed lower left: "Degas"
Belvedere, Vienna, Inv.-Nr. 3846

Tina BLAU-LANG
Springtime in the Prater, 1882
Oil painting on linen
214x291 cm
signed lower right: "Tina Blau / Vienna
1882"
Belvedere, Vienna, Inv.-Nr. 2233

Claude MONET
Fishermen on the Seine near Poissy, 1882
Oil painting on linen
59.8x81.7 cm
signed lower richt: "Claude Monet / Poissy 1882"
Belvedere, Vienna, Inv.-Nr. 1288

Claude MONET
The Chef (Monsieur Paul), 1882
Oil painting on linen
64.5x52.1 cm
signed above right: "Claude Monet 82."
Belvedere, Vienna, Inv.-Nr. 540

Pierre Auguste RENOIR
Bather with long, blonde hair, around 1903
Oil painting on linen
92.7x73.4 cm
signed lower right: "Renoir" (legacy stamp)
Belvedere, Vienna, Inv.-Nr. 2414

Lovis CORINTH
Still life with chrysanthemums and amaryllis, 1922
Oil painting on linen
121x96 cm
Frame measurements: 154x130x9 cm
signed lower left: LOUIS CORINTH / 1922
Belvedere, Vienna, Inv.-Nr. 2446

Olga WISINGER-FLORIAN
Poppies in bloom, around 1895-1900
Oil painted on paperboard
70x98 cm
lower left: Wisinger Florian
Belvedere, Vienna, Inv.-Nr. 8139

Theodor von HÖRMANN
Field of sainfoins near Znaim, 1893
Oil painting on linen on wood
22x48 cm
unsigned
Belvedere, Vienna, Inv.-Nr. 1202

Carl MOLL
The Naschmarket in Vienna, 1894
Oil painting on linen
86x119 cm
signed lower left: "C.Moll 1894"
Belvedere, Vienna, Inv.-Nr. 252

Emil Jakob SCHINDLER
February landscape (Pre-spring in Vienna
Woods), 1884
Oil painting on linen
120x96 cm
signed lower right: "Schindler" (legacy stamp)
Belvedere, Vienna, Inv.-Nr. 5228

Max LIEBERMANN
Hospital gardens in Edarn,
1904
Oil painting on linen
70.5x88.5 cm
signed lower left:
"M. Liebermann 1904"
Belvedere, Vienna, Inv.-Nr.
629

Claude MONET
Path in Monet's Garden in Giverny, 1902 (detail)
Oil painting on linen
89,5 x 92,3 cm
signed lower right: „Claude Monet 02"
Belvedere, Vienna, Inv.-Nr. 3889

HISTORISM

The expansion of the imperial residence city of Vienna reached its zenith with the building of the Ringstrasse. Furnishing and appointing the numerous Ringstrasse palais structures and public buildings such as the Imperial Opera House, Imperial Museums, Burgtheater, Beaux Arts Academy and the Musikverein, awoke the need for a suitably representative style. Public monuments soon ornamented the larger city squares as well. Anton Dominik Ritter von Fernkorn's equestrian statue of Prince Eugene of Savoy quickly won high popular acclaim, together with another of his monuments for the Heldenplatz square.

The Belvedere collection houses the nation's largest and most important assemblage of paintings from the era of Historism. It was Salzburg painter Hans Makart more than any other who placed his stamp upon this epoch in the 1870s and 1880s. His atelier was a magnetic enticement to visitors, his latest paintings the talk of the town. Makart's works combine the artistic virtuosity of Paolo Veronese, the sensuousness of Peter Paul Rubens and a pompous joy in theatrical staging. It was no coincidence that the large-scale 1873 painting known as "Triumph of Ariadne" was originally designed as a stage curtain for Vienna's erstwhile Comic Opera. Above all else, Makart was a master of feminine portraits; he loved to have the ladies of bourgeois society pose for him in historical costumes, as the 1879 portrait "Bertha von Piloty" graphically illustrates.

Painter Hans Romako, unlike the successful Hans Makart, fought in vain for recognition in Viennese society. The style Romako pursued pioneered the way towards the future; its hallmark was an exaggerated realism, as evidenced in his 1883 work, "The Rosebud Picker". A further unusual work based on a specific historical event is Anton Romako's "Admiral Tegetthoff in the Sea Battle near Lissa," which captures the decisive moment of the adversarial maritime attack.

During the Makart era, painter Anselm Feuerbach of Heidelberg was appointed Professor of Visual Arts at the Wiener Akademie in 1871. He was the antithesis of Makart, a pillar of the academic-classic school of painting. He created the monumental ceiling painting of the Academy's auditorium. At the same time, oriental motifs were much in fashion, as demonstrated by numerous vivid depictions of exotic bazaars by the so-called "Egyptian painter" Leopold Carl Müller. And then, the rural, peasant milieu of the alpine regions also supplied popular motifs. The Munich artist Franz von Defregger produced some of his most beloved works in this genre.

It was not until after the death of the prince of painters, Hans Makart, in 1884 that the young Gustav Klimt, his brother Ernst Klimt and their academy confrere Franz von Matsch aligned to establish a painters' association which subsequently executed numerous decorative commissions for an array of stage sets in the style of Makart, both in Vienna and elsewhere in the lands of the monarchy. One example of the elegant style of these young painters is "Young Couple in the Garden", which Ernst Klimt painted in 1890, depicting newlyweds in historic costumes.

Anton Dominik Ritter von FERNKORN
Equestrian statue of Prince Eugene François of
Savoy
(1663-1736), 1862
bronze
60x37x62 cm
right rear: A.v. Fernkorn fecit / Vienna 1862.
Belvedere, Vienna, Inv.-Nr. 4032

Anselm FEUERBACH
Self-portrait with cigarette, 1871
Oil painting on linen
62.5x49.5 cm
signed upper left: "A.Feuerbach s.ips.R 71"
Belvedere, Vienna, Inv.-Nr. 2093

Theodor FRIEDL
Cupid and Psyche, around 1890
marble
height: 193 cm
unsigned
Belvedere, Vienna, Inv.-Nr. 5903

Hans MAKART
Bertha von Piloty, née Hellermann
(1838-1872), 1872
1879
Oil painting on linen
126x92.5 cm
unsigned
Belvedere, Vienna, Inv.-Nr. 5503

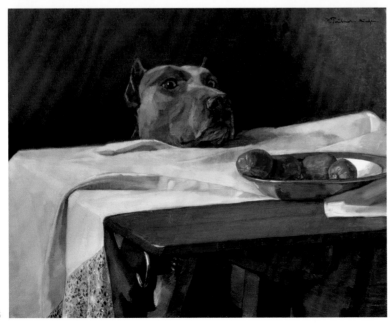

Wilhelm TRÜBNER
Caesar at the Rubicon (The artist's dog)
around 1878
Oil painting on linen
48.5x61.5 cm
upper right: "W.Trübner München"
Belvedere, Vienna, Inv.-Nr. 8522

Franz von DEFREGGER
The Last Contingent, 1874
Oil painting on linen
139x191 cm
signed lower right: "F.Defregger / 1874"
Belvedere, Vienna, Inv.-Nr. 2551

Wilhelm (Maria Hubertus) LEIBL
Head of a farmer girl, around 1880
Oil painted on wood
30x27.5 cm
signed upper right: "Leibl", upper left: "{B}
erbling."
Belvedere, Vienna, Inv.-Nr. 594

Hans MAKART
Charles V's (1500-1558) entry into Antwerp, 1875
Oil painting on linen
127x240 cm
unsigned
Belvedere, Vienna, Inv.-Nr. 4453

Leopold Carl MÜLLER
Market in Cairo, 1878
Oil painting on linen
136x216.5 cm
signed lower right: "Leopold Carl Müller. 1878."
Belvedere, Vienna, Inv.-Nr. Lg 353

Anton ROMAKO
The Rosebud Picker, around 1883
Oil painting on linen
89x66 cm
signed lower left: "A.Romako / Geneve"
Belvedere, Vienna, Inv.-Nr. 1832

Carl SCHUCH
Large kitchen still Life, 1879
Oil painting on linen
160x183 cm
signed lower right: "C. Schuch"
Belvedere, Vienna, Inv.-Nr. 1095

Ernst KLIMT
Young couple in the garden
(Paolo and Francesca), around 1890
Oil painting on linen
125x95 cm
Belvedere, Vienna, Inv.-Nr. 9528

Anton ROMAKO
Admiral Tegetthoff in sea battle
near Lissa I, around 1878
1880
Oil painted on wood
110x82 cm
signed upper right: "Tegetthoff bei Lissa /
rennt die Corazzata / Re d
'Italia ein./A. Romako"
Belvedere, Vienna, Inv.-Nr. 5032

VIENNA IN 1900

Both in Austria and abroad, the domain "Viennese Art in 1900" remains the most well known component of the Belvedere collection. Many works from this epoch go back to the very beginnings of the Belvedere as a "modern art gallery". The "Vereinigung bildender Künstler Österreichs Secession" ("Association of Artists of the Austrian Secession") which was founded in 1897 purchased scores of works by local and foreign artists which were presented at their own exhibitions, such as Hodler's "Ergriffenheit" ("Emotion") or Vincent van Gogh's "Plain of Auvers", in order to further the successful development of a modern museum. The principle of merging Austrian art into an international mainstream can also be attributed to the Secession. This feature permitted visitors to view outstanding international artists such as Van Gogh, Liebermann, Monet, Jawlensky, Nolde and others adjacent to the highlights of local artists.

Symbolism brought a new zest to the evolution of stylistic art. Artists oriented towards symbolism rebelled against depicting pure and simple reality, their pictorial world was one of feelings and instincts, of eros and thanatos. In that spirit, they used colours that alienated observers, they simplified depiction, they gave flat, two-dimensionality priority over illusionism. Both Hirémy-Hirschis's 1898 painting "Souls on the River Acheron" and Karl Meditz's painting "Loneliness - a motif from Lacroma" are examples of this.

In the final analysis, the most important local proponent of symbolism is doubtless Gustav Klimt, who through paintings such as "Liebespaar" ("Loving Couple") - better known under the title "The Kiss" - created one of the most famed paintings in the world. Gustav Klimt's most important theme was "woman", depicted (sometimes excessively) both in symbolic paintings as well as via stylisation and through the use of symbolic ornaments. There is a certain secretiveness which seems to lie behind the 1898 painting "Portrait of Sonja Knips". The lady portrayed gazes at the viewer steadfastly and seriously, the delicate, pink-toned web of her fashionable dress lends the painting a certain incorporeality. Just a few years later, Klimt painted one of his most famous women's portraits, in 1901, his rendering of "Judith". In this work, Klimt paid tribute to the myth of the seductive, erotic, and at the same time utterly unpredictable woman. Finally, the "Portrait of Fritza Riedler" of 1906 inimitably demonstrates the combination of abstract Jugendstil decor and precise realism. The formal harmony and Klimt's psychological sensitivity have made this woman's portrait both fascinating and irresistible ever since.

Klimt's landscape paintings were made during the summer months, which the artist usually spent on Lake Attersee, together with the Flöge family. Klimt was not in the slightest interested in topographical depiction in these landscape paintings, but rather chose to depict close-up sections, for example of a meadow covered with flowers. The flowers extend all the way to the edge of the painting, thus calling to mind the effect of a large scale ornamental design. The painting "Blooming Poppies" of 1907 also achieves this luminary effect.

Gustav Klimt was one of the key figures in the explosion of artistic life in Vienna before 1897, which until then was firmly anchored in traditions. During this year, a group of artists broke away from the Künstlerhaus under his aegis and founded the Wiener Secession. Besides Klimt, of whom the world's largest collection of paintings is in the Belvedere, many other Belvedere painters also belonged to the Secession, including Koloman Moser, Carl Moll, the craftsman Josef Hoffmann and architects Otto Wagner and Joseph Maria Olbrich. These artists developed a concept of spatial art whose goal was to merge architecture, visual arts and handicrafts into a harmonious unity. As of 1910, Koloman Moser dedicated himself exclusively to painting after intensive work as a designer for the Wiener Werkstätte, which he himself helped to found, and created imposing works, such as the "Self-Portrait" of 1916-17.

Between 1898 and 1905, the Wiener Secession put on a total of 24 large scale exhibitions in which a new ideal of art was propagated from the very first moment: progress and internationality. In the foreword of the first exhibition catalog it was stated, almost programmatically: "Since the public at large has abandoned itself to sweet ignorance with regard to the powerful art movement abroad, we have made great efforts in our first exhibition to present a picture of modern foreign art so that the public will benefit from higher standards for purposes of evaluating local productions." In 1905, a rupture occurred in the Secession and its leading artists, together with Klimt, abandoned the association.

At the same time, the bell had tolled the end of the Viennese Jugendstil. A young generation, with Egon Schiele and Oskar Kokoschka at the forefront, took over the leadership. Schiele shows a certain indebtedness to Jugenstil art, nevertheless changes his paintings in expressionistic ways, as the "Portrait Eduard Kosmack" vividly illustrates. Schiele's portraits are invariably marked by certain strident gestures and facial expressions. The contest between Schiele and Klimt is visually most evident in his interpretation of the loving couple in the painting "Tod und Mädchen" ("Death and Young Girl"), which - contrary to Klimt's "The Kiss" - is a pessimistic and melancholic depiction of a sexual relationship.

At the same time, Schiele's paintings are famous for their passion and for the artist's utterly liberated attitude towards the sexuality of man and woman. One of the key works in the oeuvre of Schiele is doubtless the painting "The Embrace", which the artist painted in 1917. It depicts a loving couple in a deeply passionate embrace. As his means of expression, Schiele utilizes graphic depiction above all else, with particular emphasis on contours and structures.

Richard Gerstl can be seen as the great renewer. He figured prominently in the circle of Viennese musicians around Arnold Schönberg. He ignored the Jugenstil style and on his own found his way to a physical, gestural expressionism. His "Portrait of Ernst Diez" of 1907, which was painted under the pronounced influence of Norwegian painter Edvard Munch, among others, further evolves a surprisingly modern concept of portrait painting.

Gustav KLIMT
Sonja Knips (1873-1959),
née Sophie Amalia Maria Freifrau Potier des Echelles, 1898
Oil painting on linen
141x141 cm
signed lower right: "GUSTAV / KLIMT"
Belvedere, Vienna, Inv.-Nr. 4403

Giovanni SEGANTINI
Evil Mothers, 1894 (detail)
Oil painting on linen
105x200 cm
signed lower right: "G.Segantini 1894"
Belvedere, Vienna, Inv.-Nr. 485

Adolf HIREMY-HIRSCHL
Souls on Acheron, 1898
Oil painting on linen
215x340 cm
lower right: "A.HIREMY (HIRSCHL) 98"
Belvedere, Vienna, Inv.-Nr. 942

Gustav KLIMT
After the rain (Garden with chickens in St. Agatha), 1898
Oil painting on linen
80x40 cm
signed lower right: "GUSTAV / KLIMT"
Belvedere, Vienna, Inv.-Nr. 374

Fernand Edmond Jean Marie KHNOPFF
Half figure of a nymph ("Vivien"), 1896
plaster, painted in colour, in gilded wooden base
height: 99 cm
signed on right leg: "FERNAND / KHNOPFF"
upper right: "VI / VI / EN"
Belvedere, Vienna, Inv.-Nr. 4431

Carl MOLL
Twilight, 1900
Oil painting on linen
80x94.5 cm
lower left: (unclear) C.M
Belvedere, Vienna, Inv.-Nr. 5879

Ferdinand HODLER
Emotion, 1900
Oil painting on linen
115x70.5 cm
signed lower right: "F.Hodler"
Belvedere, Vienna, Inv.-Nr. 1942

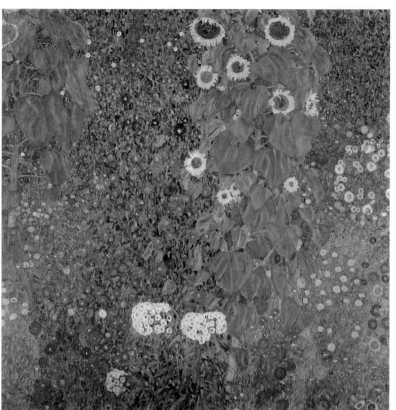

Gustav KLIMT
Farmer's garden with sunflowers,
around 1906
Oil painting on linen
110x110 cm
signed lower left: "GUSTAV / KLIMT"
Belvedere, Vienna, Inv.-Nr. 3685

Franz von MATSCH
Hilda and Franz von Matsch,
the artist's children, 1901
Oil painting on linen
120x105 cm
on the frame: Hilda und Franzi Matsch 1901
Belvedere, Vienna, Inv.-Nr. 6205

Gustav KLIMT
Judith I, 1901 (detail)
Oil and gilding on linen
84x42 cm
signed lower left: "Gustav / Klimt",
on the upper frame:
"JUDITH UND / HOLOFERNES"
Belvedere, Vienna, Inv.-Nr. 4737

Elena LUKSCH-MAKOWSKY
Adolescentia, 1903
Oil painting on linen
171x78 cm
lower right: ELM 1903
Belvedere, Vienna, Inv.-Nr. 5948

Constantin MEUNIER
The Load Carrier, 1905
bronze
225 cm
signed on foot plate: "C.Meunier", on rear base
founder's stamp: "B.VERBEYST.FONDEUR./BRUXELLES"
Belvedere, Vienna, Inv.-Nr. 764

Gustav KLIMT
Water snakes (Girlfriends I), 1904-1907 (detail)
Mixed technique, gold on parchment
50x20 cm
lower right: GUSTAV / KLIMT
Belvedere, Vienna, Inv.-Nr. 5077

Edvard MUNCH
Painter Paul Hermann and Dr. Paul
Contard, 1897
Oil painting on linen
54x73 cm
lower left: E.Munch 97
Belvedere, Vienna, Inv.-Nr. 3838

Wilhelm BERNATZIK
Pond, around 1900
100x71 cm
signed lower left: "Wilh. Bernatzik"
Belvedere, Vienna, Inv.-Nr. 6557

Gustav KLIMT
Fritza Riedler (1860-1927), née Friederike Langer, 1906
Oil painting on linen
152-134 cm
signed on left side: "GUSTAV / KLIMT / 1906"
Belvedere, Vienna, Inv.-Nr. 3379

Karl MEDIZ
Loneliness (Motif from Lacroma),
around 1902-1903
Oil painting on linen
132x184 cm
unsigned
Belvedere, Vienna, Inv.-Nr. 542

Richard GERSTL
Art historian Prof. Dr. Ernst Diez
Oil painting on linen
184x74 cm
unsigned
Belvedere, Vienna, Inv.-Nr. 4036

Gustav KLIMT
The Kiss (Loving Couple), 1907-1908 (detail)
Oil, silver and gilding on linen
180x180 cm
signed lower right: "GUSTAV / KLIMT"
Belvedere, Vienna, Inv.-Nr. 912

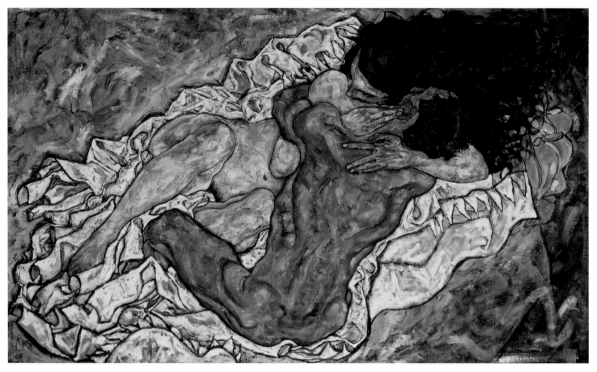

Egon SCHIELE
The Embrace (Loving Couple II, Man and Woman), 1917
Oil painting on linen
100x170 cm
unsigned
Belvedere, Vienna, Inv.-Nr. 4438

Egon SCHIELE
Four trees
(Chestnut allee in autumn;
Landscape with four
trees), 1917
Oil painting on linen
111x140 cm
signed lower right:
EGON / SCHIELE / 1917
Belvedere, Vienna, Inv.-Nr. 3917

Gustav KLIMT
Blooming poppies, 1907
(detail)
Oil painting on linen
110x110 cm
signed lower right:
"GUSTAV / KLIMT"
Belvedere, Vienna,
Inv.-Nr. 5166

Egon SCHIELE
House wall (Window wall), 1914
Oil painting on linen
111x142 cm
personally signed on stretcher frame,
reverse side:
"Eigentum Hans Böhler, Wien I,
Elisabethstr. 12"
Belvedere, Vienna, Inv.-Nr. 4278

Gustav KLIMT
Upper Austrian Farmhouse, 1911
Oil painting on linen
110x110 cm
other: 125x125x13 cm protective glass
signed lower right: "GUSTAV / KLIMT"
Belvedere, Vienna, Inv.-Nr. 1370

Egon SCHIELE
Publisher Eduard Kosmack, 1910 (detail)
Oil painting on linen
100x100 cm
center: S.10
Belvedere, Vienna, Inv.-Nr. 4702

Koloman (Kolo) MOSER
Blossoming shrub, 1913
Oil painting on linen
99.5x50 cm
lower left: KM (intertwined) / 1913
Belvedere, Vienna, Inv.-Nr. 4632

Anton HANAK
Young Sphinx (also: Maiden, Eve, Virgin, Young Eve), 1916
marble
height: 187 cm
on rear right side of base: ANTON HANAK 1916
Belvedere, Vienna, Inv.-Nr. 2067

Egon SCHIELE
Dr. Victor Ritter von Bauer, 1918
Oil painting on linen
141x110 cm
lower center: EGON / SCHIELE / 1918
Belvedere, Vienna, Inv.-Nr. 3158

Egon SCHIELE
Art historian Prof. Dr. Franz Martin Haber Ditzl
(1882-1944), 1917
Oil painting on linen
140x110 cm
lower right: EGON / SCHIELE / 1917
Belvedere, Vienna, Inv.-Nr. 9638

Egon SCHIELE
The Family (Crouching Couple)
1918
Oil painting on linen
150x160cm
unsigned
Belvedere, Vienna, Inv.-Nr. 4277

Gustav KLIMT
Allee in Park at Schloss Kammer
(Castle Park), around 1912
Oil painting on linen
110x110 cm
signed lower left: "GUSTAV /
KLIMT"
Belvedere, Vienna, Inv.-Nr. 2892

Albin EGGER-LIENZ
Death Dance of 1809, 1908
Casein on linen
225x233 cm
lower left: A.EGGERLIENZ / 1908;
lower left: DER TOTENTANZ VON /
ANO NEUN
Belvedere, Vienna, Inv.-Nr. 883

Egon SCHIELE
Death and the Maiden (Man and Maiden; Embracing
Persons), 1915
Oil painting on linen
150x180 cm
lower right: EGON / SCHIELE / 1915
Belvedere, Vienna, Inv.-Nr. 3171

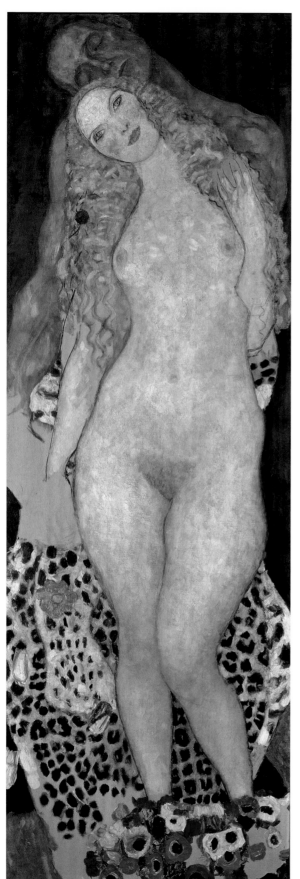

Koloman (Kolo) MOSER
Self-portrait, around 1916-1917
Oil painting on linen on cardboard
74x50 cm
unsigned
Belvedere, Vienna, Inv.-Nr. 5569

Gustav KLIMT
Adam and Eve, 1917-1918
Oil painting on linen, incomplete
173x60 cm
unsigned
Belvedere, Vienna, Inv.-Nr. 4402

Egon SCHIELE
Edith Schiele, the artist's wife, seated, 1918
Oil painting on linen
140x110 cm
lower left: EGON / SCHIELE / 1918;
on stretcher frame, reverse side right: Egon Schiele, Wien
XIII, Bildnis E. Sch. 1918
Belvedere, Vienna, Inv.-Nr. 1991

MODERN ART UNTIL 1945

At the beginning of the twentieth century, artists finally abandoned the traditional definition of art as the replication of tangible objects and nature scenes. One of the pioneers of this new way of seeing and thinking about things was Vincent van Gogh. His later works possess an incomparable aura, a brilliance and a suggestiveness which paved the way for modern art. His 1890 painting "Plain of Auvers" was created just weeks before the artist died. It was purchased in 1903 at the renowned Impressionist exhibition in Vienna by members of the Secession and given to the newly founded Modern Gallery in Vienna. Ever since then, it numbers among the most renowned paintings in the Belvedere collection.

Van Gogh exercised enormous influence on German Expressionists, among others. The Belvedere collection has works by members of the "Brücke" movement, founded in 1905, and the "Blauer Reiter" movement founded in 1911, including works by Ludwig Kirchner, Max Pechstein, Emil Nolde and Alexei von Jawlensky. Early Cubism, initiated by Picasso and Braque in Paris, is also represented at the Belvedere, through the 1912-13 work by Fernand Léger, "Village Landscape". In Austria, Max Oppenheimer adopts certain elements of Cubism early on and later develops them further in his great work, begun in 1935, "The Orchestra".

The icon of early Expressionism in Austria is Oskar Kokoschka. The Belvedere has important works from every phase in the work of this artist who died in Switzerland in 1980. First and foremost, early portraits number among the most distinguished contributions to international modern art today. The 1913 painting "Portrait of Carl Moll" depicts with a reduced palette of colours a powerful and concentrated treatment of forms.

In Austrian painting before 1945, emphasis on strong colours is typical. The main proponents of this colour expressionism are Herbert Boeckl, Anton Faistauer and Anton Kolig. More than any other, Carinthian artist Herbert Boeckl exercises far reaching influence through his emphasis on gestural, pastel painting technique. His "Self Portrait", painted in Paris in 1923, is an imposing example of how the force of gestural paint dabs can transform a traditional artistic motif. Additional important representatives of gestural painting technique are Josef Dobrowsky and Wilhelm Thöny of Graz. Expressionist painting continues to thrive in Germany until the middle of the century in the work of Max Beckmann. His 1931 painting "Reclining Woman with Book and Irises" can be cited as an outstanding specimen of that movement.

In contradistinction to impulsive and subjectively created Expressionism, the painters of the "New Objectivity" ("Neue Sachlichkeit") made valiant efforts towards emotional detachment. Precision and sobriety are the hallmarks of this movement. Important representatives include Karl Hofer in Germany and Rudol Wacker in Austria. The 1932 painting "Two Heads" by Wacker, who hailed from Vorarlberg, presents a veritable enigma with its motifs. Further exponents of the New Objectivity in Austria are Albert Paris Gütersloh, Franz Lerch and Joseph Floch.

Oskar KOKOSCHKA
Painter Carl Moll (1861-1945), 1913
Oil painting on linen
128x95.5 cm
signed lower right: OK
Belvedere, Vienna, Inv.-Nr. 4009

Alexej von JAWLENSKY
Alexej von JAWLENSKY
Self-portrait, 1912
Oil painted on cardboard, stretched onto linen
65.5x44.5 cm
unsigned
Belvedere, Vienna, Inv.-Nr. 4605

Alexej von JAWLENSKY
Portrait of a lady, around 1908
Oil painted on cardboard, stretched onto linen
65.5x44.5 cm
unsigned
Belvedere, Vienna, Inv.-Nr. 4027

Vincent van GOGH
Plain of Auvers, 1890
Oil painting on linen
50x101 cm
unsigned
Belvedere, Vienna, Inv.-Nr. 1007

Fernand LÉGER
Village landscape, 1912-1913
Oil painting on linen
91-81 cm
reverse side, upper right: F LEGER /
(1912-1913);
reverse side: Ölstudie
Belvedere, Vienna, Inv.-Nr. 2528

Alexander ARCHIPENKO
Female Nude, around 1920
bronze
height: 51.5 cm
on the pedestal: Archipenko
Belvedere, Vienna, Inv.-Nr. 2438

Emil NOLDE
Joseph tells his dreams, 1910
Oil painting on linen
86x106.5 cm
unsigned
Belvedere, Vienna, Inv.-Nr. 2409

Max PECHSTEIN
Still life with apples and china pot, 1912
Oil painting on linen
88x89 cm
lower right: HMP (intertwined)/ 1912
Belvedere, Vienna, Inv.-Nr. 4308

Ernst Ludwig KIRCHNER
The Mountains of Klosters, around
1923
Oil painting on linen
120.5x120.5 cm
lower right: E.L.Kirchner
Belvedere, Vienna, Inv.-Nr. 2475

Herbert BOECKL
Summer evening on Lake
Klopeiner, 1923
Oil painting on linen
44x52 cm
Belvedere, Vienna, Inv.-Nr. 2444

Oskar KOKOSCHKA
The Tiger, 1926
Oil painting on linen
96x129 cm
lower left: OK
Belvedere, Vienna, Inv.-Nr. 6323

Joseph FLOCH
Lily Wallis, 1923
Oil painting on linen
96.5x64 cm
lower left: Floch
Belvedere, Vienna, Inv.-Nr. 6331

Carl HOFER
Maiden with leafed plant, 1923
Oil painting on linen
105x74 cm
lower right: CH. (intertwined)
Belvedere, Vienna, Inv.-Nr. 2501

Herbert BOECKL
(Parisian) Self-portrait, 1923
Oil painting on linen
61x50 cm
Left: Meiner Maria / Paris / 16.III.23
Belvedere, Vienna, Inv.-Nr. 2443

Josef DOBROWSKY
Study hour, 1934
Oil painting on linen
101.5x118.5 cm
upper left: J Dobrowsky 34
Belvedere, Vienna, Inv.-Nr. 3312

Anton KOLIG
Kneeling Narcissus, 1920
Oil painting on linen
93x65.5 cm
unsigned
Belvedere, Vienna, Inv.-Nr. 4558

Oskar LASKE
Ship of Fools, 1923
tempera (with gilding) on linen
195x240 cm
lower left: Das Narrenschiff / op. III 2 1923
Belvedere, Vienna, Inv.-Nr. 2387

Marie Louise von MOTESICZKY
Self-portrait with comb, 1926
Oil painting on linen
83x45 cm
lower left: 1926
Belvedere, Vienna, Inv.-Nr. 9094

Rudolf WACKER
Two heads, 1932
Oil painted on wood
100x63 cm
lower right: R.Wacker 32
Belvedere, Vienna, Inv.-Nr. 3287

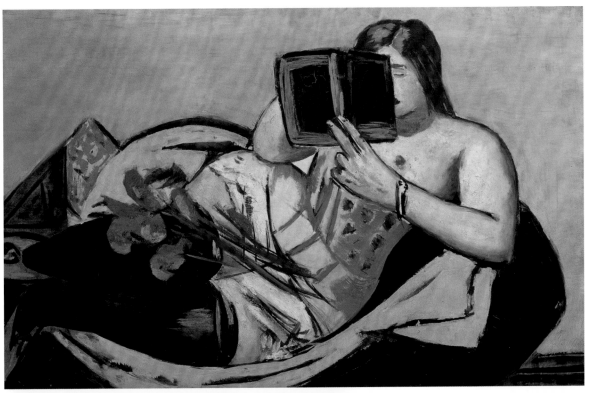

Max BECKMANN
Reclining woman with book and irises, 1931
Oil painting on linen
72.5x116 cm
lower right: Beckmann M. 31
Belvedere, Vienna, Inv.-Nr. 4120

Franz LERCH
Maiden with hat, 1929
Oil painting on linen
80x60 cm
lower right: F.Lerch 29
Belvedere, Vienna, Inv.-Nr. 6075

Albert Paris GÜTERSLOH
Alexandra Gütersloh, the artist's daughter, 1934
Oil painting on linen
60x80 cm
lower right : GÜTERSLOH 34
Belvedere, Vienna, Inv.-Nr. 3286

Karl SUSCHNIK
Boy in landscape (allegory), 1935
Oil on plywood
98x131 cm
lower right: 3 KS 5
Belvedere, Vienna, Inv.-Nr. 6042

Maximilian OPPENHEIMER
The Orchestra: Gustav Mahler conducts the Vienna Philharmonic, 1935-1952
Oil painted on wood
each 302x155 cm (triple-panel)
unsigned
Belvedere, Vienna, Inv.-Nr. Lg 813 (Leihgabe der Artothek des Bundes)

Wilhelm THÖNY
East River, New York, 1935-1938
Oil painted on heavy paper
56x78.2 cm
upper left: Thöny
Belvedere, Vienna, Inv.-Nr. 4624

Oskar KOKOSCHKA
The port of Prague, 1936
Oil painting on linen
91x117 cm
lower left: OK
Belvedere, Vienna, Inv.-Nr. 3378

Erika Giovanna KLIEN
Diving Bird, 1939
Oil painting on linen
111x96 cm
unsigned
Belvedere, Vienna, Inv.-Nr. 9547

MODERN ART AFTER 1945

The Belvedere Collection of modern and contemporary art concentrates on developments in Austrian art after the year 1960. To a great extent as a reaction to the painting and sculpture of the first half of the century, artists evolved forms of communication which were equally occupied with expressionistic tendencies as with conceptual art, minimalistic art, installation and performance art, architecture and design. Finally, reflections of the media also play a decisive role and a receive high degree of artistic attention.

The Grande Dame of Austrian art in the twentieth century is Maria Lassnig. Her works extend from informal creations of the 50s to critical examinations of the female body in recent years. The self portraits of Elke Krystufek reflect both body and sexuality in their relation to medial depiction. Franz West transforms form-fits as missing links or protheses to the theme of his early sculptures. They find their continuation in furniture pieces and space-consuming bodily forms, e.g. of Heimo Zobernig.

Since the year 2001 the Belvedere also has exhibition rooms in a special centre for contemporary art at the Augarten Contemporary. The programme of Augarten Contemporary inlcudes personal Austrian artists, e.g. Valie Export, Kurt Kren, Markus Schinwald, Constantin Luser, as well as thematic and group exhibitions such as "Objects. Austrian Sculpture after 1945", "Pictures. Photographic researches in the City", "Ulysses", "Grief", "After Schiele" (curated by Thomas Trummer) and "Form and Reason. Monika Baer. Thomas Eggerer. Amelie von Wulffen". The focus is on the close relations of local artists with the young international artist scene in particular.

In the last year alone, a series of new purchases including works by Josef Dabernig, Roland Kollnitz, Stefan Sandner, Markus Schinwald, Fabian Seitz, Martina Steckholzer, Misha Stroj and Oktavian Trauttmansdorff has been made. It is thanks to the generous gift of Thaddaeus Ropac that new works by Julius Deutschbauer, Walter Obholzer, Gerwald Rockenschaub, Hubert Scheibl and Erwin Wurm could be brought into the collection.

This repertoire of activities is further expanded by an Artist-in-Residence program. For a few months, international artists are invited to work here and participate in stimulating dialogue with the Austrian art scene. Until now, artists such as Jonathan Monk, Anne Sofi Sidèn, Jakob Kolding, Koo Jeong-a, Marcin Macieowski and Silke Otto-Knapp have been guest recipients of this program. Selected works of these artists now extend the outer dimensions of the Belvedere collection.

The quintessential aim of these developments is for the Belvedere collection to serve as the active research base of Austrian art production. In close cooperation with academies and universities in Vienna and the other states of Austria, Austrian art is being thrust into the centre of a new and ongoing discussion. Through the re-opening of the 20er Haus, which is planned for the year 2010, the Belvedere will possess yet another stage for contemporary Austrian art.

Herbert BOECKL
Woodpecker in flight II,
1950
Oil painting on linen
73x100 cm
unsigned
Belvedere, Vienna, Inv.-Nr. 5482

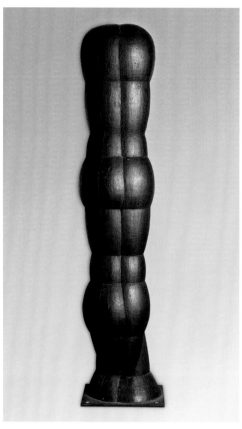

Joannis AVRAMIDIS
Standing figure, around 1960
bronze (on thin iron plate)
height: 101 cm
on lower side: Avramidis
Belvedere, Vienna, Inv.-Nr. Lg 615
(on loan from National Artothek)

Alfred HRDLICKA
The painter Oskar Kokoschka (1886-1980) II, 1963
reddish marble from Untersberg
height: 53 cm, pedestal: 0.8cm
unsigned
Belvedere, Vienna, Inv.-Nr. Lg 161
(on loan from National Artothek)

Fritz WOTRUBA
Large seated figure (Cathedral), 1949
limestone
height: 145 cm
unsigned
Belvedere, Vienna, Inv.-Nr. 4769

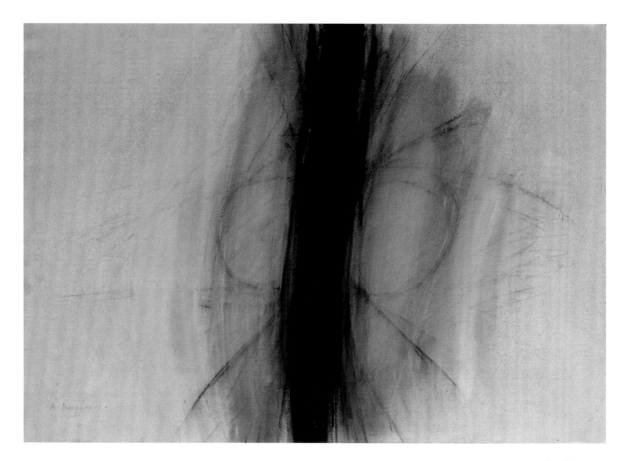

Arnulf RAINER
Vertical, 1963
mixed technique (oil chalk, oil paint,
treated with fixing spray)
73.5x105 cm
lower left: A.Rainer 63
(on loan from National Artothek)

Hubert SCHEIBL
"However, I believe we need a lot
more time to check the conditions
before we can think about making
this public"
(2001:
Odyssey in Space), 2003 / 04
Oil painting on linen
240x350 cm
Belvedere, Vienna, Inv.-Nr. 9731
(gift of Thaddaeus Ropac)

Lisl PONGER
out of austria, 2000, 2000
cprint 3#5
126x102 cm
Belvedere, Vienna, Inv.-Nr. Lg 1142

Kiki KOGELNIK
Triangle, 1975
Acrylic, Oil painting on linen
184x137.5 cm
lower left: Kiki Kogelnik 75
Belvedere, Vienna, Inv.-Nr. Lg 903
(on loan from National Artothek)

Maria LASSNIG
Double self-portrait with camera, 1974
Oil painting on linen
180x180 cm
Belvedere, Vienna, Lg 842 (on loan from National Artotheque)

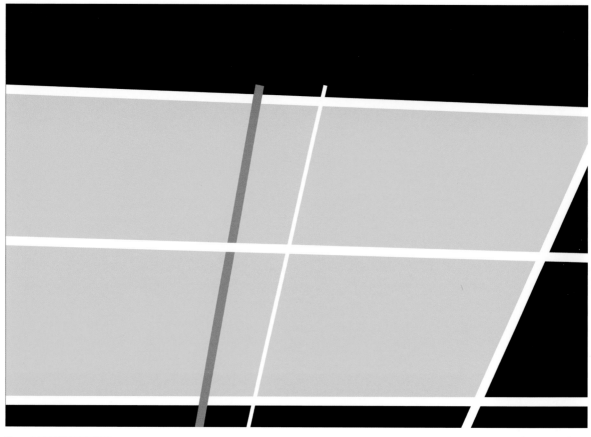

Gerwald ROCKENSCHAUB
Without title, 2000
210x300 cm, color foil on aluminum core
Belvedere, Vienna, Inv.-Nr. 9755 (Schenkung Thaddaeus Ropac)

Siegfried ANZINGER
Two warriors 1995
Acrylic on linen
258x318 cm
unsigned
Belvedere, Vienna, Inv.-Nr. Lg 1093

Erwin WURM
Without title, 2002
99x74 cm
D-Print
Belvedere, Vienna, Inv.-Nr. 9670

Hans SCHABUS
Adriatic Sea at Venice 13 May 2005, 2005
cPrint
125x147 cm
Belvedere, Vienna, Inv.-Nr. 9704

EVERYONE HAS ONE IDEA OF FREEDOM THAT ALLOWS NO
ONE ELSE TO HAVE ANOTHER.

Markus MUNTEAN
Adi ROSENBLUM
Everyone has one idea of freedom that allows no one
else to have another, 2001
Acrylic on linen
110x80 cm
lower side: EVERYONE HAS ONE IDEA OF FREEDOM
THAT ALLOWS NO ONE ELSE TO HAVE ANOTHER;
reverse side: MUN /(/ ROS /.01
Belvedere, Vienna, INv.-Nr. 9607
Belvedere, Vienna, Inv.-Nr. 9607

Elke KRYSTUFEK
Woman of Colour, 1997
Acrylic, emulsion paint on linen
140x130 cm
unsigned
Belvedere, Vienna, Inv.-Nr. 9529

PRINTING INFORMATION

Published by Agnes Husslein-Arco

Texts by: Sabine Grabner, Michael Krapf, Dietrun Otten, Veronika Pirker-Aurenhammer,
Katharina Schoeller, Franz Smola, Eva Maria Stadler

Editors: Nathalie Hoyos, Katharina Schoeller

Picture selection: Hadwig Kräutler

Picture archives: Bernhard Andergassen

Picture processing: Rudolf Hemetsberger

Graphic art: Peter Baldinger

Overall production: Alpina Druck Innsbruck

Translations: Jeffrey McCabe

Publisher Belvedere: ISBN 978-3-901508-52-3

Photo© Belvedere, Vienna 2008